SNOW WHITE MOVIE ANALYSIS

Exploring Themes, Symbolism, and Character Development in the 2025 Adaptation

Jamel Lier

© Copyright 2025 - All rights reserved.

The content contained within this book may not be reproduced, duplicated, or transmitted without direct written permission from the author or the publisher.

Under no circumstances will any blame or legal responsibility be held against the publisher, or author, for any damages, reparation, or monetary loss due to the information contained within this book, either directly or indirectly.

Legal Notice:

This book is copyright-protected. It is only for personal use. You cannot amend, distribute, sell, use, quote, or paraphrase any part, or the content within this book, without the consent of the author or publisher.

Disclaimer Notice:

Please note the information contained within this document is for educational and entertainment purposes only. All efforts have been executed to present accurate, up-to-date, reliable, and complete information. No warranties of any kind are declared or implied. Readers acknowledge that the author is not engaged in the rendering of legal, financial, medical, or professional advice. The content within this book has been derived from various sources. Please consult a licensed professional before attempting any techniques outlined in this book.

By reading this document, the reader agrees that under no circumstances is the author responsible for any losses, direct or indirect, that are incurred as a result of the use of the information contained within this document, including, but not limited to, errors, omissions, or inaccuracies.

Table of Contents

Introduction 7
Chapter 1 17
Exploring the Themes in Disney's 2025 Snow White Adaptation 17
Chapter 2 23
Cinematography: Visual Storytelling in Disney's 2025 Snow White Adaptation 23
Chapter 3 37
The Power of Symbolism in Disney's 2025 Snow White Adaptation 37
Chapter 4 46
Character Evolution in Disney's 2025 Snow White Adaptation 46
Chapter 5 56
The Music and Soundtrack of Disney's 2025 Snow White Adaptation 56
Chapter 6 63
Social and Cultural Context in Disney's 2025 Snow White Adaptation 63
Chapter 7 72
Scene-by-Scene Breakdown of Disney's 2025 Snow White Adaptation 72
Conclusion 83

Introduction

Snow White, Disney's 2025 live-action adaptation of their 1937 animated classic, marks a significant evolution in the portrayal of timeless fairy tales. Directed by Marc Webb, this version endeavors to honor the original narrative while introducing contemporary elements that resonate with today's audiences.

Overview of the 2025 *Snow White* Adaptation

The film reintroduces audiences to Snow White (Rachel Zegler), a princess whose life is upended by her father's untimely death and her stepmother's (Gal Gadot) tyrannical rise to power. Stripped of her royal status, Snow White becomes a scullery maid in her kingdom. Her inherent kindness and beauty incite the jealousy of the Evil Queen, leading to Snow White's exile into a perilous forest. There, she encounters seven dwarfs—Doc, Grumpy, Bashful, Sleepy, Sneezy, Happy, and Dopey—who work in a diamond mine. Together, they uncover the

Queen's dark secrets and rally the kingdom to restore justice.

This adaptation distinguishes itself by expanding character backstories and infusing new musical compositions by Benj Pasek and Justin Paul. The narrative delves deeper into themes of leadership, empathy, and resilience, portraying Snow White as a proactive leader inspired by her late father, rather than solely a damsel in distress.

A New Vision: What Makes This Version Unique

One of the most notable departures from previous adaptations is the reimagining of Snow White's character. Portrayed by Rachel Zegler, Snow White is envisioned as a compassionate and just leader, striving to unify her people and challenge her stepmother's oppressive rule. This portrayal emphasizes inner strength and empathy, aligning with modern values of leadership and social justice.

The film also introduces Jonathan (Andrew Burnap), a charismatic bandit who becomes Snow White's ally and romantic interest. Their evolving relationship adds depth to Snow White's character, showcasing her capacity for trust and partnership. This dynamic offers a fresh perspective on the traditional prince-charming archetype, presenting a more egalitarian partnership.

Visually, the film employs innovative filmmaking techniques, utilizing CGI to create the dwarfs and the enchanted forest. While some critics have noted that the CGI dwarfs may appear less impactful than their live-action counterparts, the film's visual style aims to blend fantasy with realism, creating a unique cinematic experience.

The narrative also addresses contemporary issues, such as the consequences of vanity and the importance of inner beauty. The Evil Queen's obsession with her appearance is a cautionary tale about the dangers of superficiality, while Snow White's journey emphasizes authenticity and kindness as true measures of beauty.

Meet the Creators: Director, Writers, and Cast

Marc Webb – Director

Marc Webb, renowned for his work on *The Amazing Spider-Man* series and the musical *500 Days of Summer*, brings a distinct directorial vision to *Snow White*. His expertise in blending character-driven storytelling with visually engaging sequences is evident in this adaptation. Webb's approach emphasizes emotional depth and narrative innovation, aiming to resonate with both new audiences and fans of the original tale.

Erin Cressida Wilson – Screenwriter

Erin Cressida Wilson, known for her work on *Secretary* and *The Girl on the Train*, crafted the screenplay for this adaptation. Her writing infuses the classic story with contemporary dialogue and complex characterizations, ensuring that the narrative appeals to a modern sensibility while honoring its origins.

Rachel Zegler – Snow White

Rachel Zegler's casting as Snow White was a subject of both excitement and controversy. At 23, Zegler, of Colombian and Polish descent, brought a fresh perspective to the character. Despite facing criticism regarding her casting, Zegler's performance was praised for its depth and authenticity. She approached the role with a focus on talent and character, emphasizing the importance of nurturing skill irrespective of appearance.

Gal Gadot – The Evil Queen

Gal Gadot's portrayal of the Evil Queen added a layer of complexity to the antagonist role. Known for her performances in *Wonder Woman* and *Fast & Furious*, Gadot embraced the challenge of depicting a character consumed by vanity and insecurity. Her performance invited audiences to reflect on the destructive nature of obsession with outward appearances.

Andrew Burnap – Jonathan

Andrew Burnap, a Tony Award-winning actor, introduced the character of Jonathan, a bandit with a heart of gold. Burnap's chemistry with Zegler added authenticity to their on-screen partnership. His portrayal highlighted themes of redemption and the transformative power of love and friendship.

The supporting cast, including actors like Ansu Kabia as the Huntsman, contributed to the film's rich tapestry, each bringing depth to their respective roles. The ensemble's collective effort ensured that the film was not just a retelling, but a reimagining that honored the essence of the original tale while adding new layers of complexity to its characters.

Final Thoughts on the Creators' Vision

The combined efforts of Marc Webb, Erin Cressida Wilson, and the talented cast brought a fresh, compelling narrative to life. Webb's direction shines through his ability to balance action with emotion, creating a film that appeals to both children and adults. Wilson's screenplay emphasizes dialogue that drives the story forward while deepening the emotional stakes for the characters. Zegler's Snow White feels authentic, empowered, and relatable, which stands in stark contrast to the passive heroine of the original 1937 animated film. Gadot's Queen, on the other hand, is more than a mere villain—she's a complex figure driven by vanity and insecurity, adding a psychological depth to her actions that invites empathy as much as disdain.

Through the creative input of all involved, the 2025 *Snow White* succeeds in bringing the classic fairy tale into the 21st century. The film not only showcases stunning visuals and updated storytelling techniques but also resonates with the current cultural climate, making it a timely adaptation of a beloved story. Whether through Snow White's leadership, the progressive re-imagining of classic tropes, or the shifting moral compass of the Evil Queen, this adaptation firmly places the tale within a modern framework, touching on themes of self-empowerment, vanity, and the transformative power of kindness.

With the collaboration of such seasoned professionals, this version of *Snow White* has become an ambitious project that is not merely a retelling, but a reinterpretation that builds upon the legacy of the original, paving the way for future generations to experience the tale in an entirely new light.

Chapter 1

Exploring the Themes in Disney's 2025 *Snow White* Adaptation

Disney's 2025 live-action adaptation of *Snow White*, directed by Marc Webb, offers a fresh perspective on the classic fairy tale, intertwining themes of empowerment, transformation, justice, and self-identity. This analysis delves into how these themes are portrayed in the film, drawing comparisons between the original 1937 animated version and the contemporary adaptation.

Empowerment and Transformation in the Modern Era

In the 2025 adaptation, Snow White (Rachel Zegler) is reimagined as a proactive and resilient leader. The film opens with a backstory where Snow White survives a snowstorm as an infant, an event that shapes her identity and resilience. Her name, Snow White, serves as a constant reminder of her survival and strength.

Throughout the narrative, Snow White transitions from a passive princess to an active leader determined to liberate her kingdom from her tyrannical stepmother, the Evil Queen (Gal Gadot). This evolution reflects modern themes of personal growth and empowerment, resonating with contemporary audiences who value self-determination and resilience. Snow White's journey emphasizes that true leadership arises from empathy, courage, and the willingness to challenge unjust systems.

The Role of Justice and Self-Identity

Justice and self-identity are central to Snow White's character development. The Evil Queen's obsession with beauty and power leads her to oppress the kingdom, highlighting the corrupting influence of vanity. In contrast, Snow White's understanding of justice is rooted in fairness and compassion. Her exile into the forest becomes a journey of self-discovery, where she learns that true beauty emanates from kindness and integrity.

Snow White's internal struggle with her identity as both a princess and a leader reflects contemporary discussions on self-realization. Her quest to reclaim her rightful place is not just about power but about restoring dignity and well-being to her people. This portrayal aligns with modern sensibilities that emphasize authenticity and the importance of aligning one's actions with personal values.

Comparing Classic and Contemporary Themes

The 1937 animated *Snow White* presents a straightforward narrative focused on beauty and the triumph of good over evil. Snow White's passivity and reliance on external rescue reflect the societal norms of its time. In contrast, the 2025 adaptation introduces complexity by exploring themes of empowerment, justice, and self-identity. Snow White's active role in her destiny and her leadership qualities resonate with modern values of gender equality and social justice.

The depiction of the Evil Queen also evolves; she is not merely a villain but a tragic figure consumed by insecurity and fear. This depth adds a layer of empathy to her character, encouraging audiences to reflect on the destructive nature of vanity and the societal pressures that fuel it.

Moreover, the 2025 film addresses contemporary issues such as representation and diversity. Casting Rachel Zegler, a Latina actress, as Snow White sparked discussions on racial and cultural representation in media. While some criticized this choice, arguing it strayed from tradition, others praised it as a step toward inclusivity. This casting decision invites audiences to reconsider traditional narratives and embrace a more diverse and representative storytelling approach.

In conclusion, the 2025 *Snow White* adaptation serves as a bridge between classic storytelling and modern values. By reimagining Snow White as a symbol of empowerment and self-discovery, the film reflects contemporary societal shifts toward equality, justice, and authenticity. This analysis underscores the importance of evolving traditional narratives to align with current cultural dialogues, ensuring that timeless tales continue to resonate with and inspire new generations.

Chapter 2

Cinematography: Visual Storytelling in Disney's 2025 *Snow White* Adaptation

Disney's 2025 live-action adaptation of *Snow White*, directed by Marc Webb, endeavors to blend classic storytelling with modern cinematic techniques. Central to this endeavor is the film's cinematography, which employs color, lighting, and camera techniques to enhance the narrative and immerse viewers in its reimagined fairy tale world.

The Art of Color and Lighting in *Snow White*

In the 2025 adaptation, color and lighting are meticulously crafted to reflect the film's evolving moods and settings. The narrative journey from Snow White's (Rachel Zegler) initial exile to her eventual return as a leader is mirrored through a dynamic color palette and strategic lighting choices.

Color Palettes: Enhancing Mood and Symbolism

The film opens in Snow White's homeland, where the color scheme is dominated by muted earth tones—browns, grays, and dull yellows. This subdued palette mirrors the kingdom's oppressive atmosphere under the rule of the Evil Queen (Gal Gadot), emphasizing themes of suppression and despair. As Snow White ventures into the enchanted forest, the colors become more vibrant, introducing lush greens and rich floral hues. This shift signifies a transition from oppression to freedom, aligning with Snow White's personal growth and the discovery of her inner strength. The forest's vivid colors also highlight the contrast between the natural world's vitality and the Queen's sterile palace. However, some critics note that while the forest is intended to be enchanting, the overuse of CGI results in a setting that feels more artificial than magical, lacking the tangible texture that might have made it more immersive.

The Queen's palace is characterized by cold, metallic tones—silvers and blacks—accentuated by sharp, contrasting lighting. This design choice reinforces the Queen's vanity and the palace's oppressive ambiance. The stark lighting within the palace casts harsh shadows, creating an atmosphere of foreboding and highlighting the Queen's tyrannical nature. In contrast, Snow White's cottage exudes warmth, with soft yellows and warm whites, achieved through gentle lighting that creates a welcoming and nurturing environment. This warmth symbolizes Snow White's inherent kindness and the sanctuary she provides amidst the surrounding darkness.

Lighting Techniques: Defining Settings and Elevating Narrative

Lighting serves as a narrative device, distinguishing various settings and reflecting character dynamics. In the forest, dappled sunlight filters through the trees, creating patterns that dance on the forest floor. This natural lighting fosters a sense of peace and freedom, aligning with Snow White's journey toward self-discovery. However, some viewers felt that the forest scenes lacked the vibrant, lively imagery expected, with the color grading appearing muted and the lighting failing to evoke the intended enchantment.

The palace scenes utilize high-contrast lighting, with sharp beams illuminating the Queen and her immediate surroundings while leaving the periphery in shadow. This technique draws focus to the Queen's actions and emphasizes her isolation from the rest of the kingdom. In Snow White's cottage, the use of warm, soft lighting creates a cozy atmosphere, enhancing the film's emotional depth and highlighting themes of hope and resilience.

Camera Techniques that Elevate the Narrative

The film's cinematography employs various camera techniques to deepen storytelling, convey character relationships, and enhance thematic elements.

Shot Composition, Angles, and Movements

Wide shots are frequently used to establish the expansive beauty of the enchanted forest, emphasizing Snow White's connection to nature and her sense of freedom. Intimate close-ups capture the nuanced expressions of characters, particularly during pivotal emotional moments, fostering a connection between the audience and the characters' internal struggles. Dynamic camera movements, such as tracking shots following Snow White through the forest, convey a sense of urgency and movement, aligning with her quest for justice and self-discovery.

Low-angle shots of the Queen in her palace convey authority and dominance, reinforcing her tyrannical rule. Conversely, high-angle shots of Snow White during moments of vulnerability evoke empathy, highlighting her resilience and growth. During action sequences, such as confrontations with the Queen's forces, the camera employs swift movements and quick cuts to heighten tension and excitement, immersing the audience in the narrative's stakes.

Aligning Camera Choices with Themes

The camera work aligns closely with the film's themes of empowerment, transformation, and justice. As Snow White transitions from a sheltered princess to a courageous leader, the camera shifts from static, composed shots to more dynamic and assertive movements, mirroring her evolution. Scenes depicting Snow White's interactions with the dwarfs are framed to emphasize unity and camaraderie, reinforcing themes of solidarity and collective action. In contrast, scenes depicting the Queen's isolation are framed with her alone in expansive, empty spaces, highlighting her detachment from the rest of the kingdom and her descent into vanity and jealousy.

How Cinematography Enhances the Story's Mood and Themes

The cinematography of the 2025 *Snow White* adaptation plays a pivotal role in shaping the film's mood and reinforcing its central themes. Through deliberate choices in color, lighting, and camera work, the film crafts an immersive experience that resonates with audiences.

Contributing to Mood: Tension, Whimsy, Darkness, and Hope

The film's visual palette fluctuates to reflect its tonal shifts. In moments of tension, such as Snow White's confrontations with the Queen, the lighting becomes stark, and shadows loom large, creating an atmosphere of suspense and foreboding. Whimsical scenes, like Snow White's interactions with forest creatures, are bathed in soft, golden light, evoking a sense of wonder and hope. The soft lighting and warm color tones during these moments create a sense of comfort, reinforcing Snow White's innocence and connection to nature. These shifts in mood are visually represented, drawing the viewer deeper into the emotional journey of the character.

Enhancing Themes of Empowerment, Transformation, and Justice

The cinematography in *Snow White* also plays a crucial role in highlighting the key themes of empowerment, transformation, and justice. As Snow White evolves from a passive character into a proactive leader, the camera techniques mirror her transformation. Early in the film, she is often framed in static, confined spaces—emphasizing her sheltered existence and lack of agency. However, as she grows, the cinematography changes to reflect her emerging strength and autonomy. Camera movements become more fluid and expansive, mirroring her journey of empowerment.

Similarly, themes of justice and moral growth are reinforced through lighting and composition. In the scenes where Snow White takes charge, the lighting softens around her, symbolizing her newfound clarity and the righteous path she follows. Conversely, the Evil Queen is often depicted in harsh, cold lighting, emphasizing her moral corruption and the destructive nature of her vanity. The contrast between the two characters, both in terms of their visual representation and their narrative arcs, underlines the central conflict between good and evil, justice and tyranny.

The use of lighting in the final confrontation scenes, where Snow White confronts the Queen, is particularly striking. The lighting shifts dramatically to represent the emotional and moral clarity Snow White has gained, and the triumph of justice over the Queen's oppressive rule. The contrast between the warm, triumphant lighting surrounding Snow White and the shadowy, oppressive environment of the Queen underscores the victory of empowerment, transformation, and justice.

Engaging the Viewer Emotionally and Intellectually

Through its cinematography, *Snow White* engages viewers not only on an emotional level but also on an intellectual one. The strategic use of camera angles, lighting, and color choices encourages the audience to reflect on the deeper themes of the story. For example, the way the film uses visual contrasts—between the warmth of Snow White's innocence and the coldness of the Queen's maliciousness—forces the viewer to confront the stark differences in their characters, reflecting the broader moral struggles depicted in the film.

The film's cinematography also invites viewers to experience Snow White's emotional journey more intimately. The close-up shots of her face during moments of vulnerability, determination, or realization allow the audience to connect with her inner turmoil and triumphs. Similarly, the wide, sweeping shots of the enchanted forest evoke a sense of freedom and possibility, contrasting with the narrow, confined spaces of the Queen's palace, which symbolize oppression and limitation.

Overall, the cinematography in the 2025 *Snow White* adaptation enhances the film's narrative and themes by using visual techniques to deepen emotional engagement and underscore the story's moral messages. Through thoughtful choices in color, lighting, and camera movements, the filmmakers create a compelling visual language that both supports and amplifies the story's emotional depth, making it a more immersive and impactful experience for the audience.

Chapter 3

The Power of Symbolism in Disney's 2025 *Snow White* Adaptation

Disney's 2025 live-action adaptation of *Snow White*, directed by Marc Webb, revisits the classic fairy tale with a modern lens, introducing nuanced symbolism that enriches the narrative. This analysis explores the traditional symbols—the apple, the magic mirror, and the forest—and examines new symbolic elements introduced in the film. We will also delve into how these symbols provide deeper insights into character development, particularly that of Snow White and the Evil Queen.

Unpacking the Classic Symbols: Apple, Mirror, and Forest

The Apple

In the original 1937 animated film, the poisoned apple serves as a pivotal plot device, symbolizing temptation and the loss of innocence. The apple's vibrant red hue is often associated with passion and desire, yet in this context, it represents the peril of succumbing to the forbidden allure. The Evil Queen's use of the apple as a disguised instrument of death underscores themes of deceit and the consequences of vanity. This symbolism aligns with broader cultural narratives where apples denote knowledge, temptation, and the fall from grace.

The Magic Mirror

The magic mirror in both the original and the 2025 adaptation represents the concept of external validation and the destructive nature of narcissism. The Evil Queen's obsession with being the fairest is a manifestation of her dependence on the mirror's affirmation, highlighting societal pressures related to beauty standards. This reliance on external approval can lead to insecurity and irrational actions, reflecting contemporary issues surrounding self-esteem and identity.

The Forest

Traditionally, the forest in fairy tales is a place of danger, transformation, and self-discovery. In *Snow White*, the forest serves as a refuge from the Evil Queen's tyranny, offering Snow White protection and a space for personal growth. This setting allows her to develop independence and resilience, aligning with modern themes of empowerment and self-actualization. The forest's duality as both a place of peril and sanctuary mirrors the complexities of real-life journeys toward self-discovery.

New Symbolism in the 2025 Adaptation

The Wishing Apple

In the 2025 adaptation, the Evil Queen presents the poisoned apple as a "wishing apple," claiming it grants the consumer's deepest desire. This reimagining adds layers to the traditional symbol, introducing themes of false hope and the manipulation of desires. It reflects contemporary concerns about the allure of quick fixes and the potential dangers of unverified promises. This twist on the classic symbol serves as a cautionary tale about the complexities of wish fulfillment and the importance of discernment.

The Mirror's Transformation

In this adaptation, the magic mirror is not just a passive reflector but an active participant in the narrative. It evolves from a simple object of vanity to a complex symbol of self-reflection and truth. This transformation aligns with modern understandings of self-awareness and the journey toward authentic self-recognition. The mirror's role challenges characters and audiences alike to confront uncomfortable truths and embrace personal growth.

The Bandit's Forest

The forest in the 2025 film is not merely a backdrop but a dynamic space where Snow White encounters Jonathan, a bandit who becomes her ally. This version of the forest introduces themes of rebellion against tyranny and the forging of unconventional alliances. It reflects contemporary values of resistance against oppression and the strength found in solidarity among diverse groups. The forest thus becomes a microcosm of the broader societal struggles for justice and equality.

What These Symbols Reveal About the Characters

Snow White

Snow White's interaction with these symbols reveals her evolution from innocence to empowerment. The apple, initially a symbol of her naivety, becomes a catalyst for her awakening to the complexities of the world. Her journey through the forest signifies her transition from dependence to self-reliance, and her relationship with the mirror represents her struggle for authentic self-recognition amidst external pressures. These symbols collectively chart her path toward leadership and self-actualization.

The Evil Queen

The Evil Queen's fixation on the mirror and the apple underscores her internal conflict and insecurity. Her reliance on the mirror's validation exposes her vulnerability to external opinions, driving her to extreme measures to maintain her perceived superiority. The wishing apple symbolizes her desperation to control outcomes, reflecting a fear of losing influence. These symbols highlight her tragic flaws and the destructive potential of unchecked vanity and obsession with power.

Supporting Characters

Characters like Jonathan, the bandit, are introduced with their symbolic associations. The forest setting of their initial meeting represents their shared desire for freedom from oppressive forces. Jonathan's character embodies themes of rebellion and solidarity, challenging traditional notions of heroism and nobility. His alliance with Snow White signifies the strength found in unity across societal divides.

Conclusion

The 2025 *Snow White* adaptation utilizes both traditional and innovative symbols to enrich character development and thematic depth. The apple, mirror, and forest retain their classic associations while acquiring new meanings that resonate with contemporary audiences. These symbols not only advance the narrative but also invite viewers to reflect on personal and societal themes of temptation, identity, and transformation. By reimagining these symbols, the film bridges the gap between classic storytelling and modern sensibilities, offering a multifaceted exploration of human nature and societal constructs.

Chapter 4

Character Evolution in Disney's 2025 *Snow White* Adaptation

Disney's 2025 live-action adaptation of *Snow White*, directed by Marc Webb, presents a reimagined narrative that emphasizes character development and modern themes. This analysis delves into the evolution of key characters, highlighting their growth, challenges, and transformations throughout the film.

Snow White: From Princess to Empowered Heroine

In the original 1937 animated classic, Snow White is depicted as a passive character, primarily defined by her beauty and kindness. The 2025 adaptation, however, transforms Snow White into a proactive and courageous leader. The film opens with a young Snow White, portrayed by Emilia Faucher, learning virtues such as fearlessness, bravery, truth, and fairness from her parents, the benevolent king and queen. These lessons are symbolized by a silver necklace engraved with these values, underscoring their significance in her upbringing.

Following the untimely death of her mother and the subsequent marriage of her father to the vain and tyrannical Evil Queen (Gal Gadot), Snow White's life takes a tumultuous turn. The Evil Queen's obsession with beauty leads her to oppress the kingdom, relegating Snow White to the status of a scullery maid. This period of adversity serves as a crucible for Snow White's character, fostering resilience and a burgeoning desire for justice.

Snow White's encounter with Jonathan (Andrew Burnap), a charismatic bandit leading a group of rebels, further catalyzes her transformation. Jonathan's influence introduces Snow White to the concepts of rebellion against tyranny and the pursuit of justice. Their alliance not only challenges her perceptions but also emboldens her to reclaim her agency and confront her stepmother's oppressive rule.

Embracing her innate leadership qualities, Snow White unites the dwarfs, rebels, and oppressed citizens in a collective uprising against the Evil Queen. This culminates in her ascending the throne, not as a figurehead defined by beauty, but as a sovereign embodying wisdom, empathy, and strength. Her journey from a sheltered princess to an empowered heroine mirrors contemporary discussions on gender roles and the reimagining of traditional princess archetypes.

The Evil Queen: A Modern Take on Villainy

The Evil Queen in this adaptation transcends the archetype of the one-dimensional villain. Portrayed by Gal Gadot, she is depicted as a complex character driven by deep-seated insecurities and an insatiable lust for power. Her fixation on being the fairest in the land stems from a profound fear of obsolescence and loss of influence, reflecting societal pressures related to aging and relevance.

Her tyrannical actions, including the subjugation of her subjects and the marginalization of Snow White, are manifestations of her internal struggles and societal conditioning that equate beauty with worth and power. This portrayal invites viewers to empathize with her vulnerabilities while critically examining the destructive nature of vanity and the societal constructs that perpetuate such obsessions.

Supporting Characters: Dwarfs, Huntsman, and More

The supporting characters in this adaptation are reimagined to reflect modern sensibilities and contribute significantly to the narrative. The seven dwarfs, traditionally depicted as comical sidekicks, are portrayed as multifaceted individuals with distinct personalities and backgrounds. Their diversity and depth enrich the story, providing Snow White with a support system that embodies a spectrum of human experiences and perspectives.

The Huntsman (Ansu Kabia), initially an agent of the Evil Queen, undergoes a transformation that parallels Snow White's journey. His internal conflict and eventual defection to Snow White's cause highlight themes of redemption and the moral complexities inherent in serving oppressive regimes. His arc underscores the possibility of change and the impact of empathy and moral courage.

Jonathan's character introduces a romantic subplot that is both empowering and egalitarian. As a leader of rebels, he challenges traditional gender roles and expectations, positioning Snow White as an equal partner in their quest for justice. Their relationship is built on mutual respect and shared goals, reflecting contemporary values of partnership and equality.

Character Arcs: Growth, Struggle, and Transformation

The film intricately weaves the character arcs of Snow White, the Evil Queen, and the supporting characters, each undergoing significant growth and transformation. Snow White's evolution from a passive princess to an assertive leader is marked by her struggles with identity, responsibility, and the weight of leadership. Her journey is a testament to resilience and the pursuit of justice.

The Evil Queen's arc, characterized by her descent into tyranny driven by insecurity, culminates in her downfall, serving as a cautionary tale about the perils of unchecked vanity and the societal constructs that uphold such values.

Supporting characters like the Huntsman and Jonathan experience arcs of redemption and empowerment, respectively. Their transformations highlight themes of morality, loyalty, and the complexities of human nature. These intertwined arcs enrich the narrative, offering a multifaceted exploration of personal and societal themes.

Conclusion

Disney's 2025 *Snow White* adaptation presents a nuanced exploration of character evolution, aligning traditional fairy tale elements with contemporary themes. The film's portrayal of Snow White as an empowered heroine, the complex depiction of the Evil Queen, and the enriched roles of supporting characters offer a fresh perspective on a classic story. These developments invite audiences to reflect on societal constructs, gender roles, and the timeless themes of empowerment and self-actualization. The character arcs in the 2025 adaptation serve as a powerful vehicle for discussing personal growth, justice, and the transformation of societal values. Through Snow White's journey, the Evil Queen's fall, and the supporting characters' evolutions, the film offers a more layered, modern take on a traditional fairy tale, one that resonates deeply with contemporary viewers.

Snow White's transformation from a passive character to an active leader challenges the conventional image of the fairy tale princess, making her a figure of empowerment for modern audiences. The Evil Queen's portrayal, rich with insecurity and vanity, serves as a poignant commentary on the destructive forces of societal pressures around beauty and perfection. Meanwhile, the supporting characters, particularly the Huntsman and Jonathan, reflect the complexity of human nature and the potential for growth, redemption, and solidarity.

In conclusion, the 2025 *Snow White* adaptation not only reimagines the fairy tale but also deepens the exploration of character development, making it a powerful and relevant story for today's viewers. The evolving characters, especially Snow White herself, represent a shift in how we view heroism, villainy, and the roles that people—especially women—can play in shaping their destinies. This approach to character evolution brings the classic story into the modern era, offering rich, relatable lessons about personal growth, leadership, and the fight for justice in a world that increasingly values authenticity and empowerment.

Chapter 5

The Music and Soundtrack of Disney's 2025 *Snow White* Adaptation

Disney's 2025 live-action adaptation of *Snow White*, directed by Marc Webb, reimagines the classic fairy tale through a contemporary lens, with music playing a pivotal role in shaping the film's tone, enhancing storytelling, and deepening character development. The collaboration between composers Benj Pasek and Justin Paul, known for their work on *The Greatest Showman* and *Dear Evan Hansen*, brings a fresh musical perspective to this adaptation.

How Music Sets the Tone for the Film

From the opening scene, the film's score establishes an atmosphere that balances the whimsical with the dramatic. The orchestration combines traditional symphonic elements with modern rhythms, reflecting Snow White's journey from innocence to empowerment. For instance, the opening number, "Good Things Grow," introduces a lively melody that captures the villagers' optimism, setting a contrast to the darker themes that unfold.

As Snow White's character evolves, so does the musical landscape. The score adapts to mirror her internal struggles and triumphs, employing leitmotifs that recur throughout the film, subtly guiding the audience's emotional responses. This technique ensures that the music not only complements the visual storytelling but also deepens the viewer's connection to the narrative.

Key Tracks and Their Emotional Impact

The soundtrack features both original compositions and reimagined classics, each serving a distinct purpose in the narrative.

- **"Waiting on a Wish"**: Snow White's introductory song encapsulates her yearning for agency and change. Rachel Zegler's heartfelt delivery conveys a sense of longing, drawing the audience into her world. This track underscores Snow White's dissatisfaction with her passive existence and foreshadows her transformative journey.
- **"All Is Fair"**: Performed by Gal Gadot as the Evil Queen, this song delves into themes of vanity and insecurity. The composition blends haunting melodies with powerful vocals, highlighting the Queen's internal conflict and obsession with beauty. The track adds depth to her character, portraying her not merely as a villain but as a figure consumed by societal pressures.
- **"A Hand Meets A Hand"**: A duet between Snow White and Jonathan, this piece symbolizes their growing alliance

and shared vision for a just world. The harmonious blend of their voices, set against a backdrop of uplifting instrumentation, reinforces the film's themes of unity and collective action.

- **"Heigh-Ho" and "Whistle While You Work"**: These reimagined classics provide moments of levity and nostalgia. The updated arrangements incorporate contemporary beats, making them resonate with modern audiences while honoring their origins. They serve as a bridge between the old and new, connecting viewers to the legacy of Disney's musical storytelling.

The Role of Sound in Enhancing Story and Atmosphere

Beyond the songs, the film's sound design plays a crucial role in immersing the audience in its world. The ambient sounds of the forest, the clinking of armor, and the bustling of village life create a rich auditory tapestry that complements the visual elements. Strategic use of silence, particularly during pivotal moments of introspection or tension, amplifies the emotional weight of the scenes.

The integration of music and sound extends to the portrayal of the film's themes. For instance, during Snow White's confrontation with the Evil Queen, the clash of their differing musical motifs underscores their ideological battle—Snow White's melodies are characterized by openness and warmth, while the Queen's are sharp and dissonant. This auditory distinction reinforces the narrative's exploration of justice, self-identity, and the corrupting influence of vanity.

In conclusion, the music and soundtrack of Disney's 2025 *Snow White* are not mere accompaniments to the story but integral components that enhance the film's emotional depth and thematic resonance. Through a thoughtful blend of original compositions and reinterpreted classics, the film offers a rich auditory experience that complements its visual storytelling, inviting audiences to engage with the narrative on a profound level.

Chapter 6

Social and Cultural Context in Disney's 2025 *Snow White* Adaptation

Disney's 2025 live-action adaptation of *Snow White*, directed by Marc Webb, reimagines the classic fairy tale to resonate with contemporary audiences. This analysis explores how the film challenges traditional gender roles, engages with modern cultural issues, and incorporates feminist themes, reflecting current social dynamics.

Breaking Stereotypes: Gender Roles and Expectations

Snow White's Transformation

In the original 1937 animated film, Snow White embodies the archetype of the passive princess, awaiting rescue by a prince. The 2025 adaptation subverts this portrayal by presenting Snow White (Rachel Zegler) as an active leader determined to liberate her kingdom from the tyrannical rule of her stepmother, the Evil Queen (Gal Gadot). This transformation aligns with modern ideals of female empowerment, depicting Snow White as a character who transcends traditional gender expectations.

Rachel Zegler's portrayal infuses Snow White with a blend of innocence and evolving strength, offering a role model for young girls that moves beyond mere passivity. This evolution reflects a broader cultural shift towards recognizing women's agency and leadership in various spheres.

Subversion of Traditional Roles

The film also reimagines other characters to challenge conventional gender norms. The Evil Queen, traditionally depicted as a one-dimensional villain, is given depth, showcasing her insecurities and the societal pressures that contribute to her obsession with beauty and power. This portrayal invites viewers to empathize with her motivations, prompting discussions about the toxic aspects of societal expectations placed on women.

Jonathan (Andrew Burnap), reimagined from the traditional prince character, emerges as a Robin Hood-like figure. His role emphasizes partnership and mutual respect, moving away from the damsel-in-distress narrative and highlighting collaborative efforts in overcoming adversity. This shift reflects contemporary values of equality and shared responsibility in relationships.

Engagement with Modern Gender Discussions

The adaptation actively engages with ongoing conversations about gender equality and female empowerment. By presenting Snow White as a proactive and self-determined leader, the film aligns with current movements advocating for women's rights and representation. However, this approach has sparked debate, with some critics arguing that the film's portrayal of Snow White as a feminist icon feels contrived, suggesting that not all female characters need to embody contemporary feminist ideals to be empowering.

Cultural Relevance in Today's World

Addressing Contemporary Issues

The 2025 adaptation addresses several cultural issues that resonate with today's audience. The Evil Queen's fixation on beauty and youth reflects societal obsessions with appearance, prompting discussions about vanity and self-worth. Snow White's journey from a sheltered princess to a leader who challenges oppressive systems mirrors global movements toward social justice and equality.

Reimagining Fairy Tales for Modern Audiences

By altering traditional elements, such as the portrayal of the dwarfs and Snow White's character, the film invites viewers to reconsider classic narratives through a modern lens. This approach aligns with a cultural shift towards inclusivity and diversity in media, acknowledging that traditional stories can evolve to reflect contemporary values.

Reflections on Beauty Standards and Diversity

The film's casting choices and character reimaginings spark conversations about beauty standards and representation. Rachel Zegler's casting as Snow White challenges conventional notions of beauty, encouraging audiences to broaden their perspectives on attractiveness and identity. This aspect of the film contributes to ongoing dialogues about diversity and representation in Hollywood.

The Feminist Undercurrent: Snow White in the 21st Century

Snow White as a Feminist Icon

Snow White's evolution in the 2025 adaptation positions her as a feminist symbol. Her transition from passivity to agency reflects feminist ideals of autonomy and self-determination. By leading a rebellion against her stepmother's tyranny, Snow White embodies the fight against patriarchal oppression, resonating with feminist movements advocating for women's rights and societal change.

Critique of Societal Pressures

The Evil Queen's character serves as a critique of societal pressures placed on women to conform to unrealistic standards of beauty and success. Her descent into obsession highlights the damaging effects of these expectations, prompting viewers to reflect on the importance of self-acceptance and the need to challenge harmful societal norms.

Debates on Feminist Representation

The film's portrayal of Snow White has ignited discussions about feminist representation in media. While some praise the depiction of a strong, independent female lead, others argue that the character's alignment with contemporary feminist ideals feels inauthentic, suggesting that the film's approach to feminism is more about adhering to current trends than offering a genuine narrative.

Conclusion

Disney's 2025 *Snow White* adaptation reflects and contributes to ongoing cultural conversations about gender, beauty, and empowerment. By reimagining traditional characters and narratives, the film challenges viewers to reconsider their perceptions of classic stories and the values they convey. However, the film also underscores the complexities involved in modernizing fairy tales, highlighting the challenges of balancing tradition with contemporary values and the diverse reactions such adaptations can provoke.

Chapter 7

Scene-by-Scene Breakdown of Disney's 2025 *Snow White* Adaptation

Disney's 2025 live-action adaptation of *Snow White*, directed by Marc Webb, offers a reimagined take on the classic fairy tale, blending traditional elements with contemporary themes. This analysis provides a detailed breakdown of key scenes, exploring their significance in character development and narrative progression, while also examining the cinematic techniques employed to enhance these moments.

Key Scenes that Define the Film

Opening Sequence: The Snowstorm and Birth of Snow White

The film opens with a dramatic depiction of a fierce snowstorm, symbolizing the tumultuous beginning of Snow White's life. Amid the storm, a queen gives birth to a daughter, Snow White, who survives the calamity. This sequence sets the tone for Snow White's resilience and foreshadows her pivotal role in the kingdom's future. The use of sweeping camera movements and intense music immerses the audience in the chaos of the storm, highlighting the miraculous nature of Snow White's birth.

The Queen's Transformation into the Evil Queen

Years later, Snow White's father marries a woman from a distant land, who, upon his absence, reveals her true nature as the Evil Queen. Utilizing dark, moody lighting and close-up shots, the film emphasizes her transformation from a seemingly benevolent stepmother to a tyrannical ruler. Her obsession with beauty and power becomes evident, setting the stage for the ensuing conflict.

Snow White's Plea for Compassion

Snow White, now a young woman, courageously approaches the Evil Queen, advocating for fair treatment of their subjects. This scene showcases her compassion and emerging leadership qualities. The contrasting lighting—Snow White bathed in soft, warm tones and the Queen shrouded in cold, harsh lighting—visually represents their differing moral compasses.

The Huntsman's Betrayal and Snow White's Flight

Ordered to execute Snow White, the Huntsman instead warns her, leading to her flight into the forest. The chase sequence is marked by rapid pacing, handheld camera work, and a pulsating soundtrack, heightening the tension and urgency of Snow White's escape.

Discovery of the Dwarfs' Cottage

Seeking refuge, Snow White discovers the cottage of seven dwarfs. The warm, inviting interior contrasts with the dark forest, symbolizing safety and new beginnings. The use of warm lighting and soft-focus lenses creates a sense of comfort, highlighting Snow White's transition from peril to protection.

The Queen's Deception with the Poisoned Apple

In a climactic moment, the Evil Queen, disguised as an old woman, offers Snow White a poisoned apple. The scene employs tight framing and a haunting musical score to build suspense, emphasizing the gravity of Snow White's impending fate.

Snow White's Awakening and Rallying the Kingdom

Following her revival, Snow White unites the dwarfs, bandits, and villagers in a rebellion against the Evil Queen. The montage of preparations is accompanied by uplifting music and dynamic editing, conveying a sense of hope and collective purpose.

Confrontation and Resolution

The final confrontation between Snow White and the Evil Queen is intense and emotionally charged. The battle is choreographed with swift movements and dramatic close-ups, capturing the stakes of the struggle. The resolution is marked by the Queen's demise and Snow White's ascension to the throne, portrayed with expansive shots and triumphant music, symbolizing renewal and justice.

Emotional Highs and Dramatic Turns

Snow White's Compassionate Leadership

Snow White's interactions with the kingdom's subjects highlight her innate leadership and empathy. Her willingness to listen and advocate for the oppressed endears her to the populace, setting her apart from the tyrannical Queen. This development is pivotal, marking her transition from a sheltered princess to a ruler attuned to her people's needs.

The Betrayal and Its Consequences

The Huntsman's initial betrayal introduces a moral complexity to the narrative. His internal conflict and ultimate decision to aid Snow White add depth to his character and underscore the themes of redemption and integrity. This twist challenges traditional notions of loyalty and justice within the story.

Snow White's Death and Rebirth

The sequence of Snow White's death and subsequent revival serves as a profound emotional pivot. It underscores the themes of hope and resilience, illustrating the enduring nature of goodness in the face of evil. This moment resonates deeply, reinforcing the narrative's emotional core.

The Climactic Battle and Its Aftermath

The rebellion against the Evil Queen culminates in a battle that tests the characters' resolve and unity. The emotional intensity of this sequence is heightened by personal stakes and the collective yearning for liberation. The aftermath brings catharsis, as the kingdom embraces a new era under Snow White's rule.

How Each Scene Contributes to the Bigger Picture

Establishing Themes of Justice and Compassion

From the outset, the film juxtaposes Snow White's inherent kindness with the Queen's cruelty, establishing a moral framework that drives the narrative. Each scene builds upon this foundation, illustrating the impact of leadership rooted in empathy versus tyranny.

Character Development and Arcs

Snow White's evolution from a sheltered princess to a wise and just ruler is meticulously crafted through her experiences and interactions. The Huntsman's journey from betrayer to ally mirrors themes of forgiveness and personal growth. The Evil Queen's descent into obsession highlights the corrupting influence of vanity and unchecked ambition.

Visual and Symbolic Cohesion

Cinematic techniques such as lighting, color palettes, and camera work are employed to reinforce thematic elements. The contrast between the warm tones of Snow White's refuge and the cold hues of the Queen's domain visually encapsulates the battle between good and evil. Symbolic motifs, like the recurring imagery of mirrors and apples, serve as visual metaphors for the characters' internal struggles and desires.

Pacing and Narrative Flow

The film's pacing, marked by moments of tension and relief, keeps the audience engaged while emphasizing the emotional weight of key scenes. The slow build-up to Snow White's death, followed by the rapid progression toward her revival and the kingdom's rebellion, creates a rhythmic balance between despair and hope. This pacing ensures that each dramatic turn feels earned and that the resolution is both satisfying and uplifting. The seamless transition between these emotional highs and lows contributes to the narrative flow, reinforcing the theme of perseverance in the face of adversity.

Each scene plays a critical role in contributing to the overall message of the film, which centers on the power of kindness, justice, and self-discovery. By carefully constructing these moments, the filmmakers ensure that the audience not only understands Snow White's transformation but also empathizes with the emotional journeys of the other characters. The film's structure, with its sharp contrasts between moments of darkness and light, highlights the cyclical nature of oppression and liberation, offering a hopeful message about the power of unity and self-realization.

Conclusion

In sum, the scene-by-scene breakdown of the 2025 *Snow White* adaptation reveals how each pivotal moment, from Snow White's flight into the forest to the climactic rebellion, contributes to the film's emotional depth and thematic complexity. The film's use of cinematic techniques such as pacing, lighting, and symbolism enhances the storytelling, ensuring that each scene resonates with audiences on both an intellectual and emotional level. The emotional highs and dramatic turns not only propel the narrative forward but also deepen the character arcs, making the ultimate victory of Snow White feel both inevitable and earned. These elements combine to create a film that is not only a reimagining of a classic fairy tale but also a powerful commentary on empowerment, justice, and personal transformation.

Conclusion

Disney's 2025 live-action adaptation of *Snow White*, directed by Marc Webb, presents a reimagined narrative that intertwines classic elements with contemporary themes. This analysis has explored how the film reflects modern societal issues, its reception compared to previous adaptations, and whether it redefines the original tale. The following sections delve into these aspects, providing a comprehensive understanding of the film's impact and significance.

What the 2025 *Snow White* Says About Today's Society

The 2025 adaptation of *Snow White* addresses several societal issues pertinent to contemporary audiences. Central themes include empowerment, identity, beauty standards, and justice.

Empowerment and Identity

Snow White's character is portrayed as a proactive leader, diverging from the passivity of the original animated version. Her journey from a scullery maid to a just ruler emphasizes themes of self-empowerment and personal growth. This evolution aligns with modern narratives that encourage individuals to take control of their destinies and challenge oppressive systems. The film positions Snow White as a symbol of resilience and determination, inspiring audiences to pursue their goals despite adversity.

Beauty Standards and Justice

The Evil Queen's obsession with beauty and her subsequent jealousy of Snow White highlights the destructive nature of vanity and the societal pressures associated with physical appearance. This portrayal invites viewers to reflect on contemporary beauty standards and their impact on self-esteem and interpersonal relationships. Additionally, the film addresses issues of social justice, depicting Snow White's efforts to rectify the injustices inflicted upon her people. Her advocacy for the oppressed resonates with current movements striving for equality and systemic change.

Gender Roles and Leadership

The adaptation challenges traditional gender roles by presenting Snow White as a capable and assertive leader. Her ability to inspire and mobilize others subverts conventional expectations of female characters in fairy tales. This portrayal aligns with ongoing cultural shifts toward recognizing and promoting women's leadership and agency in various spheres of society.

Legacy and Reception: How It Stands Among Other Adaptations

The reception of the 2025 *Snow White* has been multifaceted, with reactions ranging from acclaim to criticism.

Critical and Audience Reactions

Critics have lauded Rachel Zegler's performance as Snow White, highlighting her depth and the empowerment she brings to the character. The film's musical elements have also received positive attention, with original songs enhancing the storytelling. However, some critiques focus on the film's deviation from traditional elements, such as the portrayal of the dwarfs and changes to the storyline, which have not resonated with all viewers.

Comparison to Previous Adaptations

Compared to earlier adaptations, both animated and live-action, the 2025 film offers a unique perspective by integrating modern themes. While some adaptations have focused on visual spectacle, this version emphasizes character development and societal commentary. However, opinions vary on whether these modernizations enhance the narrative or detract from the original's charm.

Position in Disney's Remake Landscape

Within Disney's broader strategy of reimagining classic tales, the 2025 *Snow White* occupies a distinctive position. It attempts to balance respect for the original material with contemporary sensibilities. The film's approach reflects Disney's ongoing efforts to appeal to modern audiences while navigating the complexities of updating beloved stories.

Final Thoughts: Does This Film Redefine the Classic?

The question of whether the 2025 *Snow White* redefines the original tale is subjective and depends on one's perspective on adaptation and tradition.

Reinterpretation of Themes and Characters

The film reimagines central themes and characters, presenting Snow White as a more autonomous and influential figure. This shift aligns with contemporary values of gender equality and empowerment. The Evil Queen's character is explored with greater depth, offering insights into the complexities of vanity and insecurity. These reinterpretations provide a fresh lens through which to view the classic story.

Impact on the Fairy Tale Genre

By addressing modern concerns such as diversity, leadership, and self-worth, the film contributes to the evolution of the fairy tale genre. It prompts discussions about representation and the relevance of traditional narratives in contemporary society. Whether this adaptation stands as a unique work or remains tethered to its classic origins is a matter of ongoing debate among audiences and critics.

Shaping Future Adaptations

The 2025 *Snow White* serves as a case study of the challenges and possibilities of adapting classic tales for new generations. It highlights the potential for storytelling to evolve while honoring original themes. The film's reception may influence how future adaptations balance tradition and innovation, shaping the trajectory of fairy tale retellings in popular culture.

In conclusion, the 2025 *Snow White* adaptation offers a multifaceted perspective on a timeless tale, reflecting contemporary societal values while sparking discussions about tradition, representation, and storytelling. Its place in the legacy of fairy tale adaptations will continue to be evaluated as audiences engage with its reimagined narrative.

Printed in Dunstable, United Kingdom